Wha

know about

HEAVEN

... but were afraid to ask

What you always wanted to know about

HEAVEN

... but were afraid to ask

CATHERINE BUTCHER

See back of book for list of National Distributors.

Unless otherwise indicated, all Scripture references are from the Holy Bible: New International Version (NIV), copyright © 1973, 1978, 1984 by the International Bible Society.
Other quotation is marked:
CEV: Contemporary English Version, copyright © 1991, 1992, 1995 by the American Bible Society.

Concept development, editing, design and production by CWR

Cover image: SXC.HU

Printed in Finland by WS Bookwell

ISBN: 978-1-85345-444-8

Thanks especially to Adrian, Rachel and Matthew, who give me space to write ... to Caroline and Rachel who help develop and sharpen my thoughts and to Mum, Dad, Vicky and Pauline for practical help and loving support.

CONTENTS

PROLOGUE

If I find in myself a desire which no experience in this world can satisfy, the most probable explanation is that I was made for another world.

C.S. Lewis[1]

This book began with a longing for something more. I'd been a Christian for most of my forty years, but it had become a dry, almost loveless, dutiful relationship with God – more work than faith.

Then, in May 2000, I took a book on holiday. It had been on my shelf for some time, unopened; I had no great expectations of it, but I began to read *The Sacred Romance* by Brent Curtis and John Eldredge. Eldredge writes:

The best human life is unspeakably sad. Even if we manage to escape some of the bigger tragedies (and few of us do), life rarely matches our expectations. When we do get a taste of what we really long for, it never lasts. Every vacation comes to an end. Friends move away. Our careers don't quite pan out. Sadly, we feel guilty about our disappointment, as though we ought to be more grateful. Of course we're disappointed – we're made for so much more. 'He has set eternity in our hearts' (Eccl. 3:11). Our longing for heaven whispers to us in our disappointments and screams through our agony ... there is in the heart of every man, woman, and child an inconsolable longing for intimacy, beauty, and for adventure. What will heaven offer to our heart of hearts?[2]

The Sacred Romance is full of references to books, music and films which had already dripped longings into my heart. I read the pages like a thirsty nomad who had crawled out of the desert to an oasis – almost afraid to drink too much in case the refreshing supply ran out before my thirst was quenched. That book helped to reconnect the supply Jesus talked about when He met the woman at the well in Samaria:

> Everyone who drinks this water will be thirsty again, but whoever drinks the water I give him will never thirst. Indeed, the water I give him will become in him a spring of water welling up to eternal life.
>
> John 4:13–15

Just like the Samaritan woman, my heart cry was: '… give me this water …'

My longing for heaven is no longer just an occasional drip. It's always there, like a river – sometime swelling to a torrent, sometimes meandering, always moving. However, what C.S. Lewis says of longing is true:

> The books or the music in which we thought the beauty was located will betray us if we trust to them; it was not *in* them, it only came *through* them, and what came through them was longing. These things – the beauty, the memory of our own past – are good images of what we really desire; but if they are mistaken for the thing itself, they turn into dumb idols, breaking the hearts of their worshippers. For they are not the thing itself; they are only the scent of a flower we have not found, the echo of a tune we have not heard, news from a country we have never yet visited.[3]

It is those scents and sounds – the news from a country we have never yet visited – that this book aims to gather. And as a news-gatherer, I'm following the journalists' tried and tested method, asking the questions: Who? What? When? Where? Why? and How?

I hope that this book will uncover your own heart cries and leave you longing for more ... more of life itself, and its source, now and in the age to come.

NOTES

1. C.S. Lewis, *Mere Christianity* (London: Fount Paperbacks, 1977) p.118. Copyright © C.S. Lewis Pte Ltd 1942, 1943, 1944, 1952. Extract reprinted by permission.

2. B. Curtis and J. Eldredge, *The Sacred Romance* (Nashville, TN: Thomas Nelson, 1997) pp.179–181.

3. C.S. Lewis, *The Weight of Glory* (London: HarperCollins, 2001) p.31. Copyright © C.S. Lewis Pte Ltd 1949. Extract reprinted by permission.

1. WHAT'S ALL THIS TALK OF 'HEAVEN'?

He has also set eternity in the hearts of men ...

Ecclesiastes 3:11

According to the Hebrew Scriptures, 'Made for Eternity' has been stamped on our spiritual DNA, which means everyone is looking for heaven, whether they know it or not.

Not true, pollsters would claim. When a Mori poll in 2003 asked British adults if they believed in heaven, only 52 per cent said 'Yes'. Of those asked, 43 per cent said they did not believe in life after death and about a quarter (23 per cent) of the 1,001 adults interviewed believed in reincarnation. In contrast, across the Atlantic, an ABC News poll in 2005 showed that 89 per cent of Americans believe in heaven.

Has British cynicism squashed hopes of heaven in half the population? Certainly advertisers still bank on potential customers having heavenly aspirations, but have Britons given up on eternity, convinced that the best life has to offer is only a more heavenly existence here and now? With half the population believing in heaven and a quarter of those polled by Mori believing in reincarnation, are a quarter facing the only other conclusion: death is the end; there is no afterlife?

Faced with a stark question from a phone-line pollster, it might seem easy to answer 'No!' to the question 'Do you believe in heaven?' But, when a loved-one is nearing death, or illness threatens your own life, the faithful and the faithless are more prone to doubt their long-held beliefs.

Although lottery ticket holders might not tick the

pollsters' 'I believe in heaven' box, it's that 'Made for Eternity' stamp on their hearts that makes them flutter with anticipation as the winning tickets are drawn. When the TV lottery show announces the winning combination, for a split second millions of people check their tickets and think, 'It could be me'. The flutter in their hearts might be heavily disguised, and laced with greed, but it's the hope of heaven – a better life hereafter.

It's the same when the divorced forty-something slips into a wedding dress and heads down the aisle for the second or third time. She's hoping for heaven – something more perfect, more intimate and more lasting.

When the ambitious young executive scans the job vacancies looking for the next career move, he's looking for heaven – satisfaction, fulfilment and the power to change futures.

Workaholic parents struggling to make ends meet, moving to a better area to find a good school for their kids; they're hoping for heaven – somewhere safe and secure, a heavenly home for their family.

As well as grandmothers, even some grandfathers are giving in to advertising hype to buy Olay's Total Effects Anti-Ageing Anti-Blemish Daily Moisturizer, motivated by that 'Made for Eternity' stamp on their hearts – a longing for eternal youth masks hopes of heaven.

Toddlers asking for that favourite bedtime story … again and again; teenagers forming their first band, dreaming of stardom; botanists searching tropical rainforests for undiscovered species; astronauts exploring space; pensioners booking the luxury holiday of a lifetime – they're all longing for a taste of heaven. It's our spiritual DNA that drives us forward.

The hope of heaven motivates millionaires and misers; house-proud homemakers and anxious asylum-seekers.

Poets, artists, musicians and authors gain inspiration from it. Advertisers and marketing specialists make money because of it. It's the hope of heaven that gets us up in the morning. Though we might not recognise it, humanity's heart cry through the ages has always been: 'There must be more than this!'

But perhaps hopes of heaven are simply religious 'pie in the sky when you die' fantasies. In 1844, Karl Marx described religion as 'the sigh of the oppressed creature, the heart of a heartless world, and the soul of soulless conditions ... the opium of the people'.[1] Implementing Marxist philosophies, Soviet Communists sought to destroy religion, but it was the sighs and heart cries of Russian souls that had the last word. Communism tried to stamp out all religion, belief in God and belief in the afterlife. Communism failed. Belief and faithfulness to God survived brutal and severe Soviet persecution. In one of many attempts to purge faith from the lives of Russian people, Soviet Communists demolished Moscow's Christ the Saviour Cathedral in 1931, but now a gold-domed replica graces the Moscow skyline, symbolising the enduring Russian belief in the God of heaven.

> Humanity's heart cry ... has always been: 'There must be more than this!'

Anthropologists identify legends in every culture which point to heaven. Don Richardson, who has spent a lifetime studying different cultures said,

> I learned recently of belief in India about *an upside-down tree* – a tree that is upside-down because it is *rooted in heaven*. That tree's branches reach down to earth,

bearing fruit for mankind. The trunk of the upside-down tree, moreover, has been *gashed*. Sap bleeding from the wound in the side of the upside-down tree offers healing to mankind.'[2]

Richardson says he is constantly surprised to learn of legends and beliefs like this in cultures around the globe, which he can use to help people identify their own deep longing for the God of heaven who makes a difference to lives here and now.

In Western culture, our fairy stories point to a heavenly happy-ever-after. Snow White, Cinderella and Sleeping Beauty are all waiting for their prince to come; Dorothy and Toto run away in search of a better life 'somewhere, over the rainbow' in *The Wizard of Oz*; and in more contemporary tales like *Toy Story*, Buzz Lightyear's heavenward – if not heavenly – goal is to go 'To infinity and beyond!' Buzz wants more of life than he has.

Nature also points us to an illusive beauty and irrepressible life – earthly echoes of an eternal heaven. The patterns of nature which have inspired great art, music and literature, all suggest that there is more to life. From the dawn chorus burst of birdsong and the unstoppable surge of spring after winter, to the ceaseless tides and innumerable stars, for those with eyes to see and ears to hear, nature cries out, 'Life cannot be stamped out! There is more …'

… the cry for justice calls out for an end to evil and a new beginning

Even in unspeakably dark places, where humanity has been crushed by evil until almost every hint of beauty or intimacy has been removed, the cry for justice calls out for an end to evil and a new beginning; a place where there are no more tears, where all wrong will be put right. In the face of wickedness and inhumanity, slaves in America sang not just for justice and freedom, but for a heavenly home, with songs like:

> Swing low, sweet chariot,
> Coming for to carry me home,
> Swing low, sweet chariot,
> Coming for to carry me home.
>
> I looked over Jordan, and what did I see?
> Coming for to carry me home,
> A band of angels coming after me,
> Coming for to carry me home ...[3]

Humanity's hope of heaven is most easily recognised in religion – but, like all things religious, there's little agreement of what is meant by 'heaven'. Each of the major faiths believe in an afterlife; either a heavenly destination or continued existence in another form.

In Islam, The Koran describes heaven as a garden:

> This is the Paradise which the righteous have been promised: it is watered by running streams: eternal are its fruits, and eternal are its shades ... As for the righteous, they shall dwell in peace together amidst gardens and fountains, arrayed in rich silks and fine brocade. Yes, and we shall wed them to dark-eyed houris. Secure against all ills, they shall call for every kind of fruit; and, having died once, they shall die no more ...[4]

Heaven plays a less important part in Hinduism and Buddhism, as they emphasise reincarnation, but at least, in both, there is something more than this earthly existence.

What about Judaism? According to Rabbi Shraga Simmons at judaism.about.com, 'The afterlife is a fundamental of Jewish belief! ... From Judaism's perspective, our eternal soul is as real as our thumb. This is the world of doing, and the "world to come" is where we experience the eternal reality of whatever we've become.'

> The Bible doesn't offer a Lonely Planet Guide to the heavenly realm

In Western tradition, concepts of heaven are largely drawn from a Christian perspective – but it's not just practising Christians who anticipate an afterlife. Children grieving a lost parent are told, 'Daddy's gone to be a star in heaven', and other people who've lost a loved one are comforted with words such as those from Henry Scott Holland's poem *All Is Well*: 'Death is nothing at all,/I have only slipped into the next room ...'

For those who call themselves Christians, heaven is normally a core belief, even if their only contact with church is at weddings and funerals in their local Anglican church. The Church of England website says:

> Funeral services always raise profound questions about the meaning of life and death. Jesus himself believed in a life-giving God: 'the God of the living, not of the dead.' Christians believe that Christ's resurrection is the triumph of good over evil and of life over death and has made eternal life available to us.

All through history, Christian doctrine has wrestled with the mysteries which are known as the *Four last things*: heaven, hell, death and judgement. We know that everybody will be judged by God and the relationship between God's love and His judgement and mercy is one of the constant themes of Christian writing.

What *heaven* is like, none of us dare say too precisely but we know that we shall delight in the presence and love of God and of the whole company of heaven. Whatever is wonderful about life here on earth is only a glimpse of the glory of the life that is to come.[5]

Many people find some comfort when the priest or other minister at a funeral service reads aloud verses from the Bible in seventeenth-century language, such as: "'I am the resurrection and the life," saith the Lord; "he that believeth in me, though he were dead, yet shall he live: and whosoever liveth and believeth in me shall never die.'"

But what does it all mean? Even longstanding Christians seem vague and muddled about heaven. The Bible doesn't offer a Lonely Planet Guide to the heavenly realm. Is it possible to unravel some of the mystery surrounding heaven? What can we be precise about? What do we mean by 'heaven'? Is it the same as eternal life? What can we expect heaven to be like? And who goes there?

NOTES
1. Karl Marx, 'Contribution to the Critique of Hegel's *Philosophy of Right*' (February, 1844).
2. Don Richardson, *Eternity in their Hearts* (Regal Books © 1981, Third Edition, 2005) p.190.
3. Wallis Willis, 'Swing Low, Sweet Chariot'.
4. The Koran (Penguin Classics © 1956, Fourth Revised Edition, 1974) pp.146 and 149.
5. http://www.cofe.anglican.org/lifeevents/funerals. Extract on funerals from the Church of England website is copyright © The Archbishops' Council 2007 and is reproduced by permission.

2. HOW DO I KNOW HEAVEN EXISTS?

Heaven's Wings

When drab, stark winter scenes give way
to vibrant green and yellow spring;
when dormant seeds
push tiny leaves
through naked earth;
when grubby caterpillars
burst gossamer cocoons
and gloriously coloured butterflies break out …

… then hopes of heaven fly in human hearts.[1]

Paul, the first-century church leader, wrote to Christians in Rome, '… since the creation of the world God's invisible qualities – his eternal power and divine nature – have been clearly seen, being understood from what has been made, so that men are without excuse' (Rom. 1:20).

Paul was explaining that eternity and divinity were obvious. The world around us reveals there is more to life than this; there is a God who created all we see.

Through the centuries, people have gained inspiration from wonders like the caterpillar's transformation into a butterfly or the beauty of a hyacinth emerging from a wizened bulb. But are these glimpses of heaven or just evidence of a 'circle of life' – as much proof of reincarnation as of an eternal existence in some other realm?

Creation certainly hints at eternity, but how can we

> The world around us reveals there is more to life than this …

clarify Paul's claim? Surely, before we can prove that heaven exists, we must know that there is something – or someone – more than mere humanity.

Paul saw people around him searching for something more. When he visited Athens he found an altar inscribed 'to an unknown god'. Here's what he had to say:

> Now what you worship as something unknown I am going to proclaim to you.
>
> The God who made the world and everything in it is the Lord of heaven and earth and does not live in temples built by hands. And he is not served by human hands, as if he needed anything, because he himself gives all men life and breath and everything else.
>
> Acts 17:23–25

Like the Athenians, many civilisations have looked to created things and made them objects of worship – the Incas' worship of the sun god they called Inti, being just one example. But, like the people in Athens, the Incas didn't stop at worshipping created things. In *Eternity in their Hearts*, Don Richardson explains how Pachacuti, the Inca king who founded Machu Picchu, began to question the sun god's credentials, asking, 'If Inti is God, why doesn't he do anything *original*? And, if Inti were truly God, *no mere created thing could dim his light!*'

Richardson records the information gleaned by a Spanish priest in 1575 who collected a number of Inca 'hymns' which show: 'Pachacuti tumbled to the realization that he had been worshiping a mere thing as Creator! Bravely he advanced to the inevitable next question: If Inti is not the true God, *then who is*?'[2]

Traditions lying dormant in his own culture pointed to an answer – *Viracocha* – the name his ancestors had given to the Lord, the omnipotent Creator of all things. Pachacuti remembered that his own father, Hatan Tupac, had once claimed to receive counsel in a dream from Viracocha, who reminded Hatan Tupac that He – Viracocha – was truly the Creator of all things.

Sadly, before Pachacuti could ensure that his people recovered their long-forgotten faith in the 'ancient, remote, supreme, and uncreated' Creator of all things, the Inca civilisation was annihilated by Spanish conquistadors. But Pachacuti certainly proved Paul to be true: he recognised that there must be an eternal, uncreated God, simply from observing what has been made.

> Jesus is the One who called God His 'Father in heaven' ...

For us today, the intricacies and wonder of our planet point at least to an intelligent designer. Christianity claims that this uncreated God does not remain remote, but has revealed Himself in Jesus, born on earth fully God and fully human. No one can prove the existence of heaven, but I can point to the claims Jesus made. Jesus is the One who called God His 'Father in heaven' and said, 'I came from the Father and entered the world; now I am leaving the world and going back to the Father' (John 16:28).

Jesus also looked forward to the future when He will return '... you will see the Son of Man [a title He used to describe Himself] sitting at the right hand of the Mighty One and coming on the clouds of heaven' (Mark 14:62).

This is not the place to argue further for the existence of God, or the reliability of the Bible as a record of Jesus' life and teaching. Plenty of eminent scholars have done that eloquently and accessibly. So, I am assuming that

Jesus has revealed God to humanity, and that the Bible is a reliable record of what Jesus said. Because of Jesus' life, death, resurrection and teaching, we can believe that there is somewhere called heaven. Jesus said He came from heaven. He died, overcame death and has returned to heaven, and promises He will come again from heaven.

For those who believe neither that Jesus reveals God to us, nor that the Bible is an accurate record of His life and teaching, belief in heaven can be little more than comforting tradition or wishful thinking. Perhaps the 48 per cent of Britons who don't believe in heaven are simply being honest, though how that squares with the Census statistic that 71 per cent claim to be Christian is somewhat baffling.

Paul said, life without hope of something that outlasts this life is futile: 'Unless Christ was raised to life, your faith is useless ... If our hope in Christ is good only for this life, we are worse off than anyone else' (1 Cor. 15:17,19, CEV).

The kingdom of heaven was one of Jesus' favourite subjects

So what about reincarnation? The Bible is quite clear: 'Just as man is destined to die once, and after that to face judgment, so Christ was sacrificed once to take away the sins of many people; and he will appear a second time, not to bear sin, but to bring salvation to those who are waiting for him' (Heb. 9:27–28).

And what about people who have claimed to have had visions of heaven – some have had near-death experiences and have described sights, sounds and sensations that they associate with heaven? Recent studies have shown that one in ten people who have had a cardiac arrest report a near-death experience of seeing tunnels of light or feeling an overwhelming sense of peace before being resuscitated. Death-bed visions were not uncommon in the days before morphine masked the senses as well as pain. But none of these accounts can prove heaven to be more than hallucinations or fantasy.

Jesus is the only man in history who has paved the way for us to follow Him to an eternal home in heaven by dying and coming back to life.

Just before He died, Jesus prayed, 'Father, I want those you have given me to be with me where I am, and to see my glory, the glory you have given me because you loved me before the creation of the world' (John 17:24).

At His trial, He told Pilate, His judge and accuser, 'My kingdom is not of this world … my kingdom is from another place' (John 18:36).

The kingdom of heaven was one of Jesus' favourite subjects. Because of Jesus' life, death and resurrection, we can be confident that heaven exists.

We were made for something more – something that lasts longer than this life, and offers more than anything this life can give. All of creation cries out for it. All cultures and religions believe in it. But, the most convincing argument for the existence of heaven is that Jesus has 'been there, done that and got the t-shirt' or (in more biblical language), His death and resurrection have bought the robes of righteousness – the vital heavenly wedding clothes for His followers to wear … But more of that later.

NOTES
1. Catherine Butcher, 'Heaven's Wings' (2007).
2. Don Richardson, *Eternity in their Hearts* (Regal Books © 1981, Third Edition, 2005) p.33.

3.

WHAT

IS HEAVEN LIKE?

A GARDEN?

3. WHAT IS HEAVEN LIKE? A GARDEN?

'No eye has seen,
no ear has heard,
no mind has conceived
what God has prepared for those who love him' –
but God has revealed it to us by his Spirit.

1 Corinthians 2:9–10

In *Bart Simpson's Guide to Life* by Matt Groening, Bart asks 'Heaven vs. Hell. Which is better?' and comes up with the following:

Angelic choirs vs. heavy metal bands
Get to see Grandma again vs. never having to see Grandma again
All God's fuzzy little creature vs. Itchy & Scratchy
Dr. Suess vs. Dr Frankenstein
Peace & quiet vs. Screeching bagpipes
One big no-smoking section vs. humongous, towering walls of flames
Celestial visions vs. made-for-TV movies
The natural order of all things vs. deregulation
Fluffy clouds vs. jet back shrouds
Eternal bliss vs. endless drum solos
Milk & honey vs. fire & brimstone
Rosy-cheeked cherubs vs. tattooed biker chicks
Winnie-the-Pooh vs. Attila the Hun
The harmonious gathering of all races and creeds vs. festival seating[1]

Even if you're not a *Simpsons* fan, you can get the general impression of Bart's view of heaven. *The Simpsons* is the closest some people get to thinking through religious issues such as 'What is heaven like?' And, like the impish cartoon character Bart, they find that the starchy, goody-goody, harp-playing image of heaven that they've imbibed, doesn't quite match up to their ideal for a happy-ever-after life.

But if heaven genuinely is beyond imagination – endlessly and indescribably fulfilling beyond our wildest dreams – can we have any insights at all to answer the question 'What is heaven like?', especially when the Bible clearly forbids any exploration of life through mediums and spiritists? As Isaiah said: 'When men tell you to consult mediums and spiritists, who whisper and mutter, should not a people enquire of their God? Why consult the dead on behalf of the living?' (Isa. 8:19).

The Bible does say that *God has revealed to us by His Spirit – what He has prepared for those who love Him* (see 1 Cor. 2:9–10). Contemporary scholars sometimes approach the Bible as if it were any other ancient set of books. I am offering a description of heaven based firmly on a belief that God the Holy Spirit has been in control of the Bible's contents from its inspiration and throughout the compilation of what's called the 'canon of Scripture'. The books that make up the Bible we have today are there because God wants each of them to be part of the Spirit's revelation to us: the history books about the Hebrews; the poetry like Psalms and Song of Solomon; the four complementary Gospels, the letters to the Early Church and the prophecies – even a surprising book like Esther, which doesn't even mention God, has an important part to play in God's revelation of Himself and His plans for His people.

Heaven is sometimes described as a garden paradise.

As we've already seen in the last chapter, creation is one way that God reveals Himself – and what He's prepared for His people. When the Holy Spirit opens our eyes we can glimpse the wonder of resurrection and new life in the world around us.

Heaven isn't simply the Garden of Eden revisited. In John's revelation of what is to come, God says '... the old order of things has passed away ... I am making everything new' (Rev. 21:4–5). When God makes something new, there's a shadow of what has been, a repeating pattern, but the new creation is infinitely better. For example, Jesus' resurrection body was recognisable but different. After the resurrection, when Mary saw Jesus in the garden, she didn't recognise Him at first; she thought He was the gardener. And the couple walking to Emmaus who met Jesus didn't recognise Him until He disappeared from their sight. Jesus' new body could be touched, He could eat a meal – but He could also appear in a locked room.

> God says ... 'I am making everything new'

God does seem to use repeating patterns in history; that repetition is part of the Holy Spirit's revelation of God's plans for those who love Him. By looking at the Genesis description of Eden, accounts of Canaan – the promised land – and John's Revelation, we can catch glimpses of heaven.

Eden, Canaan and the heavenly realm described in John's Revelation are all well-watered and fruitful. The Garden of Eden – that place portrayed in Genesis which God said was 'very good' – was teeming with life; abundantly fruitful with streams bubbling up to water the ground, irrigating and refreshing without rain; a place where God walked in the cool of the day, that evening time when the perfume from flowering plants is most delightfully pungent; a place where men and women felt no shame; where there was creative and fulfilling work to do ruling over creation, prospering and reproducing abundant life.

The children of Israel caught a glimpse of the heavenly garden when they saw their promised land for the first time. Moses sent twelve men to explore the land. They returned with some of the fruit they'd found, including a single cluster of grapes so big it had to be carried on a pole between them. 'We went into the land to which you sent us, and it does flow with milk and honey! Here is its fruit' (Num. 13:27), they reported.

Canaan was obviously lush, green and full of flowering plants if it was the 'land flowing with milk and honey' that the twelve spies described. If Canaan's domesticated animals had enough to eat to make endless supplies of milk, and bees could make abundant quantities of honey, it must have been the well-watered garden later alluded to by the prophets (Isa. 58:11; Jer. 31:12). For people who had made a long journey on foot through a desert, it was a place where they could lie down in green pastures, walk beside quiet waters and be refreshed in body and soul – fulfilling a collective longing that still resonated with the Hebrew people many years later when their shepherd king, David, wrote his much-loved psalm and talked of dwelling in the house of the Lord forever (Psa. 23).

… a continually fruitful place; Eden restored

After that first trip to explore Canaan, when they were about to enter the promised land, God spoke to the

36

Israelites about the country they were about to possess. As well as explaining to them what to expect in Canaan, God gives us a glimpse of what we can expect heaven to be like.

> The land you are entering to take over is not like the land of Egypt, from which you have come, where you planted your seed and irrigated it by foot as in a vegetable garden … the land you are crossing the Jordan to take possession of is a land of mountains and valleys that drinks rain from heaven. It is a land the LORD your God cares for; the eyes of the LORD your God are continually on it from the beginning of the year to its end …
>
> I will send rain on your land in its season, both autumn and spring rains, so that you may gather in your grain, new wine and oil. I will provide grass in the fields for your cattle, and you will eat and be satisfied …
>
> Every place where you set your foot will be yours …
>
> Deuteronomy 11:10–11,14–15,24

If the thought of a garden seems bland, be assured, although this heavenly garden is full of flowering plants and abundant fruit, it won't involve mind-numbing seed-sowing, weeding and watering like the work in a vegetable garden. God will take care of that. This 'land of mountains and valleys' seems to produce an effortless and abundant harvest. We are not looking forward to a remake of Beatrix Potter's vegetable garden – this heavenly garden has the opulence and grandeur of African rainforests and Himalayan mountains. God's description suggests that the land being prepared for us will have all the thrills of an unexplored tropical island, the satisfaction of a vineyard that produces a vintage crop and delights to beat the best the Chelsea Flower

Show has to offer.

John's Revelation showed heaven to be the source of the river of life; a continually fruitful place; Eden restored:

> Then the angel showed me the river of the water of life, as clear as crystal … On each side of the river stood the tree of life, bearing twelve crops of fruit, yielding its fruit every month. And the leaves of the tree are for the healing of the nations …
>
> Revelation 22:1–2

In this garden, you don't have to wait till harvest time once a year for fruit – there's a fresh crop every month. There's healing and an end to the curse of pain and death.

For the world's agricultural communities, where food crops have to be harvested after unpredictable weather, water shortages and back-breaking work, the heavenly garden is a strong and attractive image of the age to come. For busy commuters, packed into sweaty trains or stuck in traffic jams, the image of a heavenly paradise where we can rest and relax is equally compelling. And for the Church, which sometimes seems to be barely surviving in a battle-ground, and where worship can sometimes seem to be more like work than an act of wonder – the heavenly garden seems to be a place of sheer enjoyment.

The heavenly paradise is for those with an adventurous spirit, like the Pilgrim Fathers looking for a new country, Victorian botanists seeking undiscovered species, or contemporary gardeners wanting the satisfaction of developing their own plant hybrid. It's for those who want rest at the end of a long journey, those who enjoy getting their hands dirty and seeing the fruit of their labour and for those who love majestic mountains and white-water rafting rivers, as well as meadows filled with wild flowers and fields of ripe grain rippling in a soft breeze. When the sights and sounds of these images move you, you are responding to the echoes of eternity. But, if the heavenly garden doesn't stir you ... God offers another image of heaven: a city.

NOTE

1. Matt Groening, *Bart Simpson's Guide to Life* (London: HarperCollins, 1996), pp.174–175.

A CITY - THE NEW JERUSALEM

4

4. A CITY – THE NEW JERUSALEM

Now, just as the gates were opened to let in the men,
I looked in after them;
and behold, the City shone like the sun:
the streets also were paved with gold;
and in them walked many men with crowns on
their heads,
palms in their hands, and golden harps to sing
praises ...
I wished myself among them.

John Bunyan[1]

Imagine, you've wandered through a desert for forty years, with nowhere to call home. When you arrive at your destination, there's still no rest. You have to fight to take possession of the land. Once you do, the security and permanence of the fortified capital city is very attractive. Add to that an annual family pilgrimage from the countryside into that city. It's like Christmas and all the Bank Holidays rolled into one. The whole extended family is there with people from every country, gathered for a magnificent feast, a family party to end all parties. When the Bible talks about a city, it's not talking about grimy buildings and sad, lonely people. This city is a thriving community, peaceful and secure within strong walls, built on a hill with marvellous views. And to cap it all, it's a royal city. The King lives there.

Modern cities don't often seem heavenly. Architects have tried to create 'garden cities' like Welwyn and Letchworth in England, but none comes close to the heavenly city's opulence as seen by John in his revelation of heaven:

… he carried me away in the Spirit to a mountain great and high, and showed me the Holy City, Jerusalem, coming down out of heaven from God. It shone with the glory of God, and its brilliance was like that of a very precious jewel, like a jasper, clear as crystal. It had a great, high wall with twelve gates, and with twelve angels at the gates. On the gates were written the names of the twelve tribes of Israel. There were three gates on the east, three on the north, three on the south and three on the west. The wall of the city had twelve foundations, and on them were the names of the twelve apostles of the Lamb.

Modern cities don't often seem heavenly

The angel who talked with me had a measuring rod of gold to measure the city, its gates and its walls. The city was laid out like a square, as long as it was wide. He measured the city with the rod and found it to be 12,000 stadia in length, and as wide and high as it is long. He measured its wall and it was 144 cubits thick, by man's measurement, which the angel was using. The wall was made of jasper, and the city of pure gold, as pure as glass. The foundations of the city walls were decorated with every kind of precious stone. The first foundation was jasper, the second sapphire, the third chalcedony, the fourth emerald, the fifth sardonyx, the sixth carnelian, the seventh chrysolite, the eighth beryl, the ninth topaz, the tenth chrysoprase, the eleventh jacinth, and the twelfth amethyst. The twelve gates were twelve pearls, each gate made of a single pearl. The great street of the city was of pure gold, like transparent glass.

I did not see a temple in the city, because the Lord God Almighty and the Lamb are its temple. The city does not need the sun or the moon to shine on it, for the glory of

God gives it light, and the Lamb is its lamp. The nations will walk by its light, and the kings of the earth will bring their splendour into it. On no day will its gates ever be shut, for there will be no night there. The glory and honour of the nations will be brought into it. Nothing impure will ever enter it, nor will anyone who does what is shameful or deceitful, but only those whose names are written in the Lamb's book of life.

Revelation 21:10–27

Ever wondered where birthstones come from, or the idea of a heavenly city with streets made of gold? Here they are in John's vision. And what about pearly gates? These gates of pearl are the way into the heavenly city. Pearls are made when something gritty, irritating and uncomfortable is transformed into something precious and beautiful in the hidden place of an oyster's shell. Is there something to be learned here about the way God transforms the pain and troubles of dying; like the Old Testament 'Valley of Achor' or Heartbreak Valley, which becomes a gateway to heavenly hope (Hosea 2:15)?

John's vision is packed with images and symbols. Although we can only know 'in part' (1 Cor. 13:12) on this side of eternity, there are some insights easily gleaned from John's vision. Notice the size and dimensions of this heavenly city. It's a perfect cube, symbolising perfection in every way. The frequent references to the number twelve link to the Old Testament when God's chosen people came from twelve tribes and the New Testament's twelve apostles, representing the Church. The symbols used to describe the heavenly city tell us that heaven is very beautiful, everlasting and secure with strong foundations and space for everyone – Jews and Gentiles – 'a great multitude that no-one could count, from every nation, tribe, people and language' (Rev. 7:9); everyone, that is, whose names are written in the Lamb's book of life (Rev. 21:27) – but we'll come back to that later.

In heaven there is no need for a temple as God is always present

The precise measurements of the city resemble the precise measurements of the gold-covered inner sanctuary of the Temple (1 Kings 6), where the ark of the covenant was kept, representing God's presence. In heaven there is no need for a temple as God is always present. But the book of Hebrews explains that the man-made Temple was designed specifically to show us what heaven is like.

> Every high priest is appointed to offer both gifts and sacrifices ... They serve at a sanctuary that is a copy and shadow of what is in heaven. This is why Moses was warned when he was about to build the tabernacle: 'See to it that you make everything according to the pattern shown you on the mountain.'
>
> Hebrews 8:3,5

What can this mean? If there is no temple in the heavenly city, how can the earthly Temple or tabernacle show us what heaven is like?

When my children were toddlers, one of their favourite toys was a plastic child-sized cooker with an oven, grill and hob. They played for hours with plastic pots and utensils, catering for imaginary parties. Their play cooker didn't have the power or dimensions of a real cooker, but it was a safe alternative that helped them to have fun beginning to learn a skill which they will value for the rest of their lives. The tabernacle and Temple – and some church buildings – were built to God's precise 'plans' to help us imagine what heaven is like. Not the stones or stained glass – but the symbols and relationships between God and His people, which show how we gain access to God's presence.

We're back to those repeating patterns in the Bible. Key elements in the Old Testament tabernacle in the desert and the Temple in Jerusalem, reveal aspects of heaven. In the Old Testament, only priests performed the sacred duties, but remember, all of Christ's followers are described as priests in the New Testament. In the shadow-picture – the Temple – there's a basin for priests to cleanse themselves before they go in. To gain access to the real thing – heaven – all Christ's followers need to be made clean. That's what baptism, repentance and forgiveness are about.

In the Old Testament copy of heaven, there's an altar for making sacrifices. In heaven – the real thing – the once-for-all sacrifice that gives access to heaven is Jesus. Jesus is described as the Lamb of God, linking the perfect lamb used as a Passover sacrifice in Exodus 12, with Jesus, the perfect One sacrificed to take away our sin, giving us access to heaven. That Lamb's Book of Life refers to Exodus, when the Hewbrew slaves avoided death by marking their homes with a lamb's blood. For us today, death has no hold on those who are symbolically marked by Jesus' blood – His death on the cross.

The anointing oil which set apart priests and all the items used in tabernacle and Temple worship is a symbol of the Holy Spirit who anoints Jesus' followers, setting them apart as God's worshipping people: '... God ... anointed us, set his seal of ownership on us, and put his Spirit in our hearts as a deposit, guaranteeing what is to come' (2 Cor. 1:21–22).

In the earthly copy of heaven, the priests wore special robes with precisely-made, square breastplates mounted with precious stones – one gem for each of the twelve tribes of Israel. The gems listed in Exodus 28, correspond with the precious stones which John saw in his vision decorating the heavenly city. When the priests entered the tabernacle or Temple wearing the breastplate with its symbolic gems, it was as if they were carrying all of the tribes of Israel into God's presence.

Hebrews 7 explains how the earthly copy shows us what is happening in heaven. Jesus is in heaven 'interceding': it's as if He is carrying His people as jewels on a breastplate over His heart, taking them into the presence of God. And, as priests, all Christians perform that same function – bringing the needs of the world before God in prayer.

Jesus is described in Hebrews as

> … a high priest [who] meets our need – one who is holy, blameless, pure, set apart from sinners, exalted above the heavens. Unlike the other high priests, he does not need to offer sacrifices day after day, first for his own sins, and then for the sins of the people. He sacrificed for their sins once for all when he offered himself … a high priest, who sat down at the right hand of the throne of the Majesty in heaven, and who serves in the sanctuary, the true tabernacle set up by the Lord, not by man.
>
> Hebrews 7:26–27; 8:1–2

The man-made version of the tabernacle and Temple described in Exodus 36–40 and 2 Chronicles 3–5 and again in Hebrews 9, had two sacred rooms, separated by a curtain – about nine metres high – which symbolised how sin separates people from God. Amazingly, at the moment when Jesus died on the cross, the Gospels of Matthew, Mark and Luke record: '... the curtain of the temple was torn in two from top to bottom ...' (Matt. 27:51; see also Mark 15:38 and Luke 23:45). Such a spectacular act could only have been achieved by the supernatural hand of God, dramatically demonstrating that we now have access into God's presence because of what Jesus has done.

As Hebrews explains, the tabernacle and Temple were earthly copies of heaven. When Christ died, He entered the most holy place in heaven – God's eternal presence – offering His own blood so that sins can be forgiven – not once a year as it was under the old system of priests, but once and for all.

So for those who think that heaven will be like an endless church service – heaven might come as a surprise. There is no church or temple in the heavenly city. But somehow, the Church – not the building, but the people – is the new Jerusalem, the City of God, the place where God makes His home now and in eternity.

The apostle Paul developed the city image of heaven in his letter to the non-Jewish Ephesians. He was particularly aware of the privileges of citizenship because, as well as being a Jew, he was a Roman citizen. He wrote:

> ... you were separate from Christ, excluded from citizenship in Israel and foreigners to the covenants of the promise, without hope and without God in the world. But now in Christ Jesus you who once were far away have been brought near through the blood of Christ ... you are no longer foreigners and aliens, but fellow-citizens with God's people and members of God's household, built on the foundation of the apostles and prophets, with Christ Jesus himself as the chief

cornerstone. In him the whole building is joined together and rises to become a holy temple in the Lord. And in him you too are being built together to become a dwelling in which God lives by his Spirit.

Ephesians 2:12–13,19–22

Just like the Ephesian believers, all Christians are citizens of heaven, being built together as the place where God makes His home, now and eternally. The heavenly city is perfect, indescribably beautiful, and with room for everyone from every people group. Eastern Orthodox church architects have tried to re-create places of worship which resemble the lavish gold-covered Temple of the Old Testament. The use of gold, purple, scarlet, white and blue in some church buildings are reminders of the colours used in the Temple curtain symbolising royalty, sacrifice, humanity and heaven. But the heavenly city that the Bible reveals will not be recognised by its splendid buildings or rich colours. It's a festival city. The atmosphere of celebration and vibrant community is what marks it out. It won't be like an everlasting church service – but a street party in a city with golden streets and no sorrow or mourning; where those who have felt like foreigners and aliens are included. This amazing place is as awesome as a throne room, but as intimate as a bridal suite. No wonder, when John Bunyan tried to imagine the pilgrims who had arrived at the heavenly city, he wrote, 'I wished myself among them'.

> ... all Christians are citizens of heaven

NOTE

1. John Bunyan, *The Pilgrim's Progress* (London: Penguin Classics, 1987).

5. A CORONATION OR A ROYAL WEDDING?

Now I saw in my dream that these two men went in
at the gate;
and lo, as they entered, they were transfigured;
and they had raiment put on that shone like gold ...
Then I heard in my dream, that all the bells in the City
rang again for joy;
and that it was said unto them, 'Enter ye into the joy
of your Lord.'

John Bunyan[1]

What is heaven like? Coronations and weddings offer some special insights. Britain's monarchy and its rich traditions are firmly based in the Christian Bible. The ceremonies and symbols which stir the heart of the nation, resonate with eternal Christian images and principles, and are a useful tool in imagining what heaven is like.

When the Queen was crowned on 2 June 1953, she arrived at Westminster Abbey in scarlet robes which emulate Christ's sacrifice. She wore a simple, white linen robe as she was anointed, showing that her reign is a gift from God not an earned or inherited right, and she left the Abbey wearing purple which indicates royalty. The colours, crowns and swords used in the coronation ceremony are each Christian symbols. Trumpets, anthems and the cheers of the crowds, recognising the start of the monarch's reign, are all part of the ceremony – shadows of what the apostle John said we can expect in heaven. When people from many races, nations and languages stand together in Westminster Abbey to witness a coronation, the whole event echoes scenes described in John's Revelation, which says that people from every race will stand before God's throne. The feelings of awe, mixed with excitement and celebration, are faint echoes of what God's people will feel as heaven unfolds.

Can you imagine being at the centre of such a ceremony? The Bible talks of all God's people receiving crowns: a crown of beauty instead of ashes (Isa. 61:3); a crown that will last forever (1 Cor. 9:25); a crown of righteousness (2 Tim. 4:8); the crown of life (James 1:12; Rev. 2:10); and the crown of glory that will never fade away (1 Pet. 5:4). But the overall impression given in Scripture is that these crowns are given while Jesus' followers are still alive; as a Christian I believe that I have already received a 'crown of life' – life that starts now and continues through eternity. Maybe that's an aspect of what Jesus meant when the Pharisees asked Him when the kingdom of God was coming and He said 'the kingdom of God is within you' (Luke 17:21).

> Can you imagine being at the centre of such a ceremony?

There's a dimension of heaven which begins as soon as people become Christians, but the Bible also suggests that there is more to come; not a coronation, but a wedding. The focus of John's vision was not on what Christians will receive, but on Jesus, His glory and His bride. In his revelation, John described a great multitude shouting loudly, announcing the impending wedding of Christ and the Church:

Hallelujah!
For our Lord God Almighty reigns.

> Let us rejoice and be glad
> and give him glory!
> For the wedding of the Lamb has come,
> and his bride has made herself ready.
> Fine linen, bright and clean,
> was given her to wear.

Revelation 19:6–9

John also describes the wedding procession seen in his vision. The 'Holy City' – also depicted as Christ's Body, the Church – is described as 'a bride beautifully dressed for her husband'. As she comes down out of heaven, John hears a loud voice proclaiming a new unity between God and humanity: '… the dwelling of God is with men, and he will live with them' (Rev. 21:3).

Weddings were a recurring theme in Jesus' parables when He taught His disciples about the kingdom of heaven. Jesus' first miracle took place at a wedding. If weddings and heaven were linked in His mind – as they clearly were in His parables – then we can expect heaven to be like the best saved till last, like that wine at the wedding in Cana.

I read a quirky story on a church website about a young woman who had grasped this 'best saved till last' principle. She had been diagnosed with a terminal illness and had been given three months to live. So she contacted her preacher and invited him to her house to discuss her final wishes. When the preacher was preparing to leave, the young woman suddenly remembered something very important to her: 'There's one more thing,' she said excitedly … 'I want to be buried with a fork in my right hand.'

The preacher stood looking at the young woman, not knowing quite what to say.

The young woman explained. 'In all my years of attending church socials and potluck dinners, I always remember that when the dishes of the main course were being cleared, someone would inevitably lean over and say, "Keep your fork". It was my favorite part because I knew that something better was coming ... like velvety chocolate cake or deep-dish apple pie. Something wonderful, and with substance! So, I just want people to see me there in that casket with a fork in my hand and I want them to wonder "What's with the fork?"

'Then I want you to tell them: "Keep your fork ... the best is yet to come."'

When Jesus told His parables about weddings, the ceremony was just the beginning of a marriage relationship. The best was still to come. In the New Testament the apostle Paul paints a picture of the Church as Christ's bride and describes the relationship as 'a mystery', linked to the mystery of a man and a woman becoming 'one flesh' (Eph. 5:25–32). Many Christians have been reticent about this heavenly family image. Controversy over gender issues in the Church and the Roman Catholic concept of Mary as 'mother of God and queen of heaven', may be the reason the image of heaven as a family has been largely ignored in Protestant churches. But, if Paul is correct, and the marriage of a man and woman is a picture of the relationship between Christ and the Church, we can't ignore the fact that the marriage in heaven marks the start of a new intimate relationship between Christ and the Church, where Paul's image of the Church as a fully functioning body with its interdependent parts, will be fleshed out.

... then we shall see face to face

As Paul said in his definition of love: 'Now we see but a poor reflection as in a mirror; then we shall see face to face. Now I know in part; then I shall know fully, even as I am fully known' (1 Cor. 13:12). 'Knowing' for someone like Paul from a Jewish background, was much more of a creative intimate relationship than our cerebral head-knowledge type of knowing in contemporary Western culture.

Another part of the Bible linked to this wedding theme, and which helps to answer the question 'What is heaven like?' is the Song of Songs. This very adult analogy can be read as King Solomon's passionate love song for his bride, but it also reveals the passion of Christ for His bride, the Church.

> You have stolen my heart, my sister, my bride;
> you have stolen my heart
> with one glance of your eyes ...
> How delightful is your love, my sister, my bride!
> How much more pleasing is your love than wine,
> and the fragrance of your perfume than any spice!
> Song of Songs 4:9–10

It is as if we are living in the preparation time, when Christ and the Church are engaged to be married; the wedding invitations have been written; the Holy Spirit and the Church are co-operating together to give that invitation to all. Using a different analogy: '... God's people ... are being built together to become a dwelling in which God lives by his Spirit' (Eph. 2:19,22). Remember, Jesus Himself described this preparation phase when He told His followers He was going to prepare a place so they could be with Him.

But one day the preparations will be over. The building

phase will be complete. The wedding arrangements will be finished. Like the bride and groom looking forward to the day when their love will be consummated and they will be one, Jesus looked forward to the day when all His followers will be united with Him and with His heavenly Father: Jesus prayed 'that they [all believers] may be one as we are one: I in them and you in me' (John 17:22–23).

The bride in Song of Songs responds to the bridegroom: 'Let my lover come ...' just as John's Revelation says:

> The Spirit and the bride say, 'Come!' And let him who hears say, 'Come!' Whoever is thirsty, let him come; and whoever wishes, let him take the free gift of the water of life.
>
> Revelation 22:17

NOTE
1. John Bunyan, *The Pilgrim's Progress* (London: Penguin Classics, 1987) pp.140–141.

6.

A VICTORY PARADE

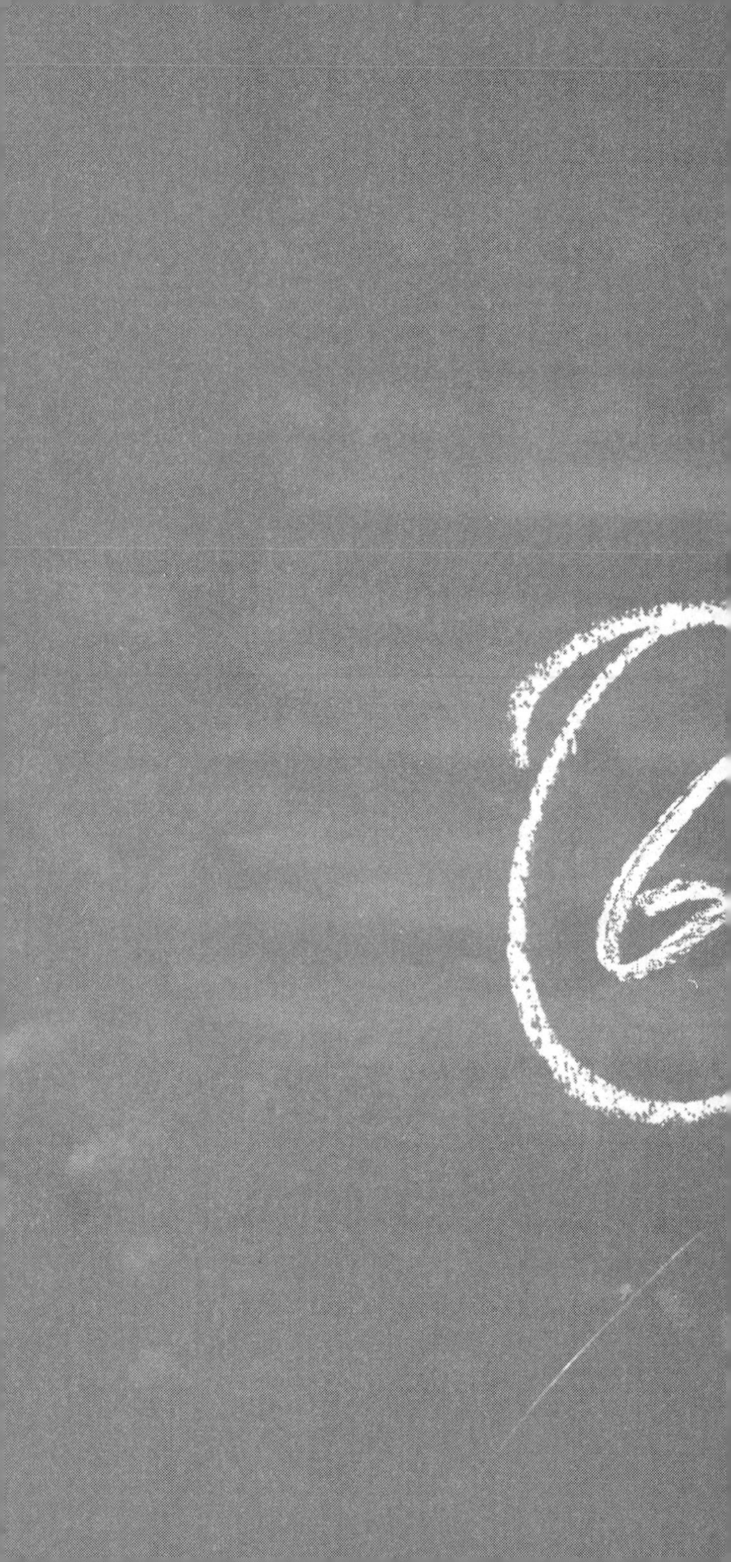

6. A VICTORY PARADE

Mine eyes have seen the glory of the coming of the Lord;
He is trampling out the vintage where the grapes of wrath
  are stored;
He hath loosed the fateful lightning of His terrible
  swift sword;
His truth is marching on.

Glory! Glory! Hallelujah! Glory! Glory! Hallelujah!
Glory! Glory! Hallelujah! His truth is marching on.

He has sounded forth the trumpet that shall never
  call retreat;
He is sifting out the hearts of men before His
  judgment seat;
Oh, be swift, my soul, to answer Him! be jubilant,
  my feet;
Our God is marching on.

He is coming like the glory of the morning on the wave,
He is wisdom to the mighty, He is honor to the brave;
So the world shall be His footstool, and the soul of wrong
  His slave,
Our God is marching on.

Julia Howe[1]

This stirring hymn was written to the tune of *John Brown's Body* by Julia Howe in 1861, during the American civil war. It was sung at the funerals of Britain's wartime Prime Minister Winston Churchill, American senator Robert Kennedy, and American presidents Ronald Reagan and Richard Nixon. The hymn takes up another of the Bible's pictures of heaven. Here heaven opens not to a garden or city, or with a wedding, but with a victory parade – the end of the last battle and the beginning of Christ's eternal reign of peace.

The Old Testament describes one battle after another; success or failure did not depend on who had the strongest army – but entirely on God. In one battle, King Jehoshaphat's army was told: 'Do not be afraid or discouraged because of this vast army. For the battle is not yours, but God's … You will not have to fight this battle. Take up your positions; stand firm and see the deliverance the LORD will give you' (2 Chron. 20:15,17). They were obedient, and their enemy was routed.

… He is still loving and forgiving …

The Israelites' experiences resemble every person's relationship with God: as we work with Him and are obedient, all is well. Even when we face life's difficulties, we have the security of knowing that God is with us, working out His good plans in our lives. Then we get complacent and compromise. God reminds us of the Maker's instructions for optimum living. We face a choice – get back into a good relationship with God or ignore Him and face the consequences. Even when we are in rebellion, God is working through all of our circumstances to enable us to return to Him. But we ignore Him and make a mess of life until, like the Prodigal Son, we come to our senses and return, repentant, to our heavenly Father. Then we discover He is still loving and forgiving; He has been waiting with outstretched arms to welcome us back; in fact, He throws a party to celebrate our return.

The Israelites took this circular route time and time again. Daniel was a prophet, a dream-reader who wrote during one of those 'facing the consequences' times in

Hebrew history. The Hebrews had been taken captive and were living in exile in Babylonia – an ancient land now part of modern-day Iraq. Daniel was longing to return home. His dreams in Daniel 10–12 had contemporary implications for his people, but also looked forward to an eternal homecoming after a last great battle, when God will bring the 'rebellion–repentance–return to God–reconciliation' cycle to an end:

> Multitudes who sleep in the dust of the earth will awake: some to everlasting life, others to shame and everlasting contempt. Those who are wise will shine like the brightness of the heavens, and those who lead many to righteousness, like the stars for ever and ever.
>
> Daniel 12:2–3

The Hebrew people faced literal battles, but also the daily battles we all face to survive in body, mind and spirit. The whole of the Bible – Old and New Testaments – sets out God's rescue plan, from humanity's first rebellion and its consequences, through God's dramatic, personal intervention through Jesus' birth, death and resurrection, to the last battle, judgment and a new age of peace. Jesus looked forward to the war to end all wars when He told His disciples:

> You will hear of wars and rumours of wars … Nation will rise against nation, and kingdom against kingdom. There will be famines and earthquakes in various places. All these are the beginning of birth-pains … this gospel of the kingdom will be preached in the whole world … and then the end will come …
>
> Matthew 24:6–8,14

For the grand finale, Jesus said:

> They will see the Son of Man coming on the clouds of
> the sky, with power and great glory. And he will send his
> angels with a loud trumpet call, and they will gather his
> elect from the four winds, from one end of the heavens
> to the other.
>
> Matthew 24:30–31

In this book about heaven, we won't be tackling the various interpretations of those last days. To my mind, that's in God's hands, rather like the last few days of a pregnancy and birth. When I was expecting our first child, my husband and I went to classes to discuss different approaches to giving birth; how to pack for the hospital; how to cope with the pain of childbirth; how to write a birth-plan. When the time came, the process was out of our hands. Rachel was born by emergency caesarean and a week later we were home with her, alone, realising we'd made detailed plans for a one-off event. We had no training or experience as parents – but this was what it had all been about: not just a birth, but a lifetime. Theologians can debate end-time theology, but this book is about eternity hereafter, not the birth pains.

The apostle Paul knew that all of the Christian life is a battle. He told the Ephesians:

> Put on the full armour of God … For our struggle is not
> against flesh and blood, but against the rulers, against
> the authorities, against the powers of this dark world and
> against the spiritual forces of evil in the heavenly realms.
>
> Ephesians 6:11–12

Paul had a strong sense of purpose and urgency, and often compared the Christian life to a race – a battle to win an eternal prize. He told the Philippian church:

> I want to know Christ and the power of his resurrection and the fellowship of sharing in his sufferings, becoming like him in his death, and so, somehow, to attain to the resurrection from the dead.
>
> Not that I have already obtained all this, or have already been made perfect, but I press on to take hold of that for which Christ Jesus took hold of me … Forgetting what is behind and straining towards what is ahead, I press on towards the goal to win the prize for which God has called me heavenwards in Christ Jesus.
>
> Philippians 3:10–14

Paul … often compared the Christian life to a race

He returned to the battle theme, linking it to heaven, when he told Timothy, 'Fight the good fight of the faith. Take hold of the eternal life to which you were called …' (1 Tim. 6:12).

Many of our epic tales and best-loved films also take up this battle theme: Tolkein's *Lord of the Rings* ends with a battle, a victory parade and a wedding; C.S. Lewis's *The Lion, the Witch and the Wardrobe* ends with a battle and a coronation and the *Narnia* series ends with *The Last Battle*. When the story ends and the characters reach Narnia's equivalent of heaven, the unicorn sums up what the rest are feeling: 'I have come home at last! This is my real country! I belong here. This is the land I have been looking for all my life, though I never knew it till now …'[2]

We are not always aware of where our sense of purpose and urgency in life comes from. We think we are longing for the perfect holiday destination, the perfect job, the perfect relationship, when these are only shadows of the beauty, satisfaction and intimacy we long for and which we will only find in heaven.

Patriotism is an echo of that longing, which makes men and women willing to die for their country.

In *Braveheart*, the heart-stirring, but highly-fictionalised version of a period in Scottish history, William Wallace rallies the reluctant Scottish troops to fight for their freedom in the face of an apparently unbeatable English army. In the Imperial War Museum's re-creation of the First World War trenches we are reminded that, in real life, men were willing to go 'over the top' in the face of apparently unbeatable odds, to fight for Britain's freedom. Longing even for shadows of heaven, makes men and women willing to fight and even to die – especially when they believe they know that death is not the end. Perhaps the twentieth century decline in patriotism and the rise of its ugly counterfeit, nationalism, is linked to the loss of that eternal certainty and a rise of humanist efforts to make the best of what we have, because we think there's nothing hereafter.

Will heaven be boring?

Heaven promises to be the end of all battles: the bloody battles of war, but also the daily battles against difficult circumstances, persecution or our own weaknesses. The hope of heaven is worth dying for, and many Christians have been martyred and are still being put to death today, because they refuse to reject their faith in Christ (see *Cox's Book of Modern Saints and Martyrs*).[3]

At the end of life's battles, heaven promises to be a

victory parade beyond our imagination, celebrating the defeat of death and the start of Christ's eternal reign of peace and justice.

So what have we learned about what heaven is like? A garden, a city, a royal wedding and a victory parade: different images of heaven – that place Jesus described as His Father's house where there are 'many rooms'.

He told His disciples, 'I am going there to prepare a place for you' (John 14:2). What will it be like? From the Bible's pictures of heaven, Jesus' followers can expect it to be a place where all our needs will be met by God's abundant provision. We will be fed – feasted even and we will be secure with an opulent palace, not a hovel, for a home. We will be with Christ and will see God face to face – without shame – as we'll be wearing the 'robes of righteousness'. Any fears we might have will be removed and our longing for intimacy – to know God and to be known by Him – will be satisfied.

… But what will we do? Will heaven be boring?

In the book *City of Gold,* writer Adrian Plass describes a discussion he had about heaven. He says:

> Surely the essence of all those beautiful things in the world must be there because they're part of him and part of us. I reckon anything good and innocent and beautiful down here has a chance of surviving in some form up there

Describing what happened next, Plass writes:

> … there was one chap, let's call him Jim, who had said nothing. Jim was a man who really loved Jesus but his language and general conversation in this context tended

to be abstract and rather unimaginatively Bible-based. He listened to our discussion with a little smile of gentle scepticism on his face.

'It's quite a thought, isn't it,' said someone else, 'that we might be allowed to do or have the very thing we've always wanted most and never been able to have?' I was just about to answer when I noticed the smile had gone from Jim's face. In its place was an expression of what appeared to be deep longing. Rarely have I seen anyone with as much of his heart in his eyes as I saw in Jim's at that very moment … 'Penny for 'em, Jim,' I said.

'Oh!' he seemed to come to with a start. 'I was just thinking how much I've always wanted …' The far-away look came back into his eyes. 'I was just thinking how absolutely wonderful it would be if he would let me have, well a lathe of my own …'

Somewhere in heaven a note was made.[4]

If heaven resembles Eden, we will have fulfilling work to do. If we are drawing on the image of heaven as a city – Jesus' parable of the talents (Matt. 25:14–30) says that those who are 'faithful with a few things' will be put in charge 'of many things'. Writing about eternal glory, Paul told Timothy 'we will also reign with him' (2 Tim. 2:12). We can only speculate as to what this might mean, but it doesn't sound boring. For those who know from their long experience of a successful marriage, how love can deepen and mature, we can only imagine what it will be like '… to grasp how wide and long and high and deep is the love of Christ, and to know this love that surpasses knowledge … [to be] filled to the measure of all the fullness of God' (Eph. 3:18–19). And if heaven starts with a victory parade, then perhaps the true freedom and peace we have fought for will finally be ours to enjoy.

The Golden City

Soon your trials will be over,
Offered up by mercy's hand;
A better view from where you're standing,
A doorway to another land.

The sweetest welcome from the Father,
Gathered up and carried home,
We are past the time of waiting,
Come let us bow before Your throne.

We will meet in the Golden City,
In the new Jerusalem
All our pain and all our tears will be no more.
We will stand with the hosts of heaven
And cry, 'Holy is the Lamb',
We will worship and adore You evermore.

Never can the powers of darkness,
Neither death, nor even life
Let nothing ever separate us
From the holy love of God.[5]

NOTES

1. Julia Howe, 'Mine Eyes Have Seen The Glory' or 'Battle Hymn of the Republic'.
2. C.S. Lewis *The Last Battle* (Lions, 1980). Copyright © C.S. Lewis Pte Ltd 1956. Extract reprinted by permission.
3. Baroness Caroline Cox and Catherine Butcher, *Cox's Book of Modern Saints and Martyrs* (London, Continuum, 2006).
4. P.A. Baggaley, *City of Gold* (Solway, August 1996).
5. 'The Golden City' by P.A. Baggaley and I.D. Blythe, from *City of Gold* (Solway, August 1996). Used with permission.

7. WHO GOES THERE?

> After this I looked and there before me was a great
> multitude that no-one could count, from every nation,
> tribe, people and language, standing before the throne
> and in front of the Lamb ... And they cried out in a
> loud voice:
> 'Salvation belongs to our God, who sits on the throne,
> and to the Lamb.'
>
> Revelation 7:9–10

Have you ever had one of those 'open heaven' experiences?
It's as if everything has fallen into its perfect place;
the jigsaw is complete and the picture is revealed; the
orchestra has finished tuning up, all the instruments
are playing one harmonious note and you know, 'This is
what they were made for'. When Eric Liddell, the Olympic
gold medallist, said 'When I run, I feel His pleasure,' he
was describing that open heaven feeling. Advertisers
promoting expensive perfume or exotic holidays work
hard to imitate open heaven moments. Even good love-
making is only a shadow of that ultimate experience.
These open heaven times are only echoes – the 'news
from a country we have never yet visited',[1] which C.S.
Lewis wrote about.

One memorable open heaven moment for me gives a
glimpse of an answer to the question: Who goes there? It
was during worship at the end of an international media
conference. Christian journalists and broadcasters from
around the world had gathered to praise God together,
each in our own language. As we sang John Newton's
famous hymn *Amazing Grace*, it was as if heaven was
open and we were part of that great multitude from every
nation, tribe, people and language, standing before God's

heavenly throne.

The general answer to the 'Who goes there?' question is: God promises that every nation, tribe, people and language will be represented in heaven. When talking to His disciples about the end of time, Jesus said, '… this gospel of the kingdom will be preached in the *whole world* as a testimony to *all nations*, and then the end will come' (Matt. 24:14, my emphasis). No racial group has privileged access. No one is excluded because of gender, colour or country of origin. It's true that the Old Testament shows how God interacted with His 'chosen people', the Jews, and Jesus made it clear that He came first for these 'lost sheep of Israel' (Matt. 15:24). But Jesus' parables show that the invitation list has been thrown wide open:

> … it was as if heaven was open and we were part of that great multitude

Jesus spoke to them again in parables, saying: 'The kingdom of heaven is like a king who prepared a wedding banquet for his son. He sent his servants to those who had been invited to the banquet to tell them to come, but they refused …

'Then he said to his servants, "The wedding banquet is ready, but those I invited did not deserve to come. Go to the street corners and invite to the banquet anyone you find." So the servants went out into the streets and gathered all the people they could find, both good and bad, and the wedding hall was filled with guests.'

Matthew 22:1–3,8–10

If you are surprised to see that 'good and bad' people are

at this heavenly banquet, remember that access to heaven has nothing to do with our qualifications or our good deeds – and everything to do with what Jesus has done on the cross and our relationship with God as a result.

In that same parable, Jesus went on to describe a wedding guest who was not wearing the wedding clothes provided by their royal host.

> 'Friend,' he asked, 'how did you get in here without wedding clothes?' The man was speechless.
>
> Then the king told the attendants, 'Tie him hand and foot, and throw him outside, into the darkness, where there will be weeping and gnashing of teeth.'
>
> For many are invited, but few are chosen.
>
> Matthew 22:11–14

These vital heavenly wedding clothes are the designer clothes God provides, which the prophet Isaiah wrote about:

> ... he [the LORD] has clothed me with garments of salvation
> and arrayed me in a robe of righteousness
> as a bridegroom adorns his head like a priest,
> and as a bride adorns herself with her jewels.
>
> Isaiah 61:10

God has been in the designer-clothing business since He made garments of skin for Adam and Eve after they disobeyed Him; they were naked and felt ashamed for the first time in their lives. For the first time, an animal's blood was shed to cover over sinfulness. That system of blood sacrifices continued until Jesus' sacrifice to end all sacrifices. Even now, our disobedience and self-centredness stains all we do; our good deeds are like dirty rags, Isaiah said. But Jesus' self-sacrifice pays for designer wedding clothes, which cover over all good and bad deeds. That's what Christians mean when they say, 'Jesus' blood covers my sin.'

Jesus looked forward to the ultimate international gathering in heaven. The guest list has been extended to all. Heaven is for those who receive and accept the invitation and put on the wedding clothes.

Surely there must be more to it than that? We all want to know more than a general answer to the 'Who goes there?' question. We want personal guarantees, just like the rich young man who asked Jesus, 'Teacher, what good thing must I *do* to get eternal life?' (Matt. 19:16, my emphasis). Jesus didn't give him a straight answer, but first offered a definition of 'good'. Jesus knew that we all think we've got to be good enough for heaven. Certainly, the young man who had asked the question seemed well qualified, if *doing good* was *good enough* for access to heaven. He said he had kept all of God's commandments since childhood: '"Do not murder, do not commit adultery, do not steal, do not give false testimony, honour your father and mother," and "love your neighbour as yourself"' (v.18). But Jesus knew the young man's heart had been captured by his wealth; money had become his security blanket, so Jesus said: 'If you want to be perfect, go, sell your possessions and give to the poor, and you will have treasure in heaven. Then come, follow me' (v.21).

Excellent rule-keeping and good deeds did not qualify that young man for heaven. But don't misunderstand Jesus – He was not simply advocating a personal Make Poverty History campaign. The young man was probably already being a good, compassionate, generous neighbour. But Jesus knew that the man could not rely on his own rule-keeping, resources and excellent credentials to gain eternal life. To get to heaven, he needed to abandon himself to God's care rather than depending on his own means.

Another rule-keeping expert, a religious leader called Nicodemus, prompted Jesus to answer the 'Who goes there?' question with one of the best-known verses in the New Testament: '… God so loved the world that he gave his one and only Son, that *whoever* believes in him shall not perish but have eternal life' (John 3:16, my emphasis). The simple answer to the question 'Who goes to there?' is, therefore, '*Whoever* believes in Jesus'.

Jesus was throwing open the heavenly invitation to embrace all. But, in the same middle-of-the-night conversation with Nicodemus, Jesus added an exclusivity clause: '… no-one can see the kingdom of God unless he is born again' and '… no-one can enter the kingdom of God unless he is born of water and the Spirit' … 'You must be born again' (vv.3,5,7).

> … money had become his security blanket …

Nicodemus was one of a particularly religious group called the Pharisees. Jesus was making a crucial point to him, and to everyone who takes pride in being religious: rule-keeping is not the route to heaven – it's all about relationships; being born into God's family. Being 'born again' is not some new American election phenomenon, it was God's idea.

So a more specific answer to the question of who goes to heaven is: people from every tribe and nation; people who are properly dressed in designer wedding clothes Jesus gives … not the rule-keeping do-gooders, but those who have been born into God's family.

Paul, the apostle, explains that being part of God's family means God's Holy Spirit comes to live in us, giving us a foretaste of heaven. The Holy Spirit is 'a deposit, guaranteeing what is to come' (2 Cor. 5:5) – like the engagement ring before the wedding day – but more than that, because the Holy Spirit is not passively waiting for people to go to heaven. The Holy Spirit is already at work in Christians, transforming them so that they become more and more like Jesus; that's the inexplicable, supernatural aspect of heavenly citizenship.

How can we understand what God does? Are there patterns in creation, or in Scripture, to help us understand? Every spring, I like to collect frog spawn to watch the black, jelly-covered dots become frogs. I find it amazing to see how spawn becomes fish with gills, then frogs with legs. Sadly, this year, my tiny frogs drowned. Once frogs' lungs develop and their gills stop working, they need to breathe air. I'd put a rock into their tank to allow them to crawl out. But they didn't make it. They were created and equipped to live and breathe on land, but for some reason, they didn't make the transition successfully. They lived and died without ever knowing what it was like to breathe fresh air, catch flies or leap using those specially-designed, lanky legs.

> God has put eternity in our hearts – that stamp of heavenly DNA

Human lives are similar in some ways. We were made for heaven. God has put eternity in our hearts – that stamp of heavenly DNA. Jesus makes it possible for us to make the transition from earth to heaven – but some people live and die without ever knowing what they were made for.

God does not remain remote and passive, watching from a distance to see if we'll make it. In Luke 15, the Gospel writer paints three vivid pictures, which show how God is at work to rescue lost people. A shepherd with a hundred sheep loses one of them, so he leaves the ninety-nine to go in search of the one that is lost. When he finds it and returns home, he invites his neighbours and friends to celebrate with him. A woman who has ten silver coins – a treasured Middle Eastern wedding gift – loses one of them, so she searches high and low for the lost coin and celebrates with friends when it's found. And there's the father whose son demands his inheritance and leaves home, only to squander the lot, ending up destitute. When the son returns, repentant, he finds his father waiting to welcome him with outstretched arms – again there's a party to celebrate the fact that the one who was lost has been found.

Some pictures of heaven focus on the joy of finding Jesus: the man who found a priceless pearl and gave up everything so he could own it; or another who found buried treasure in a field and sold everything he had to buy that field. These stories show how we might react on discovering the amazing life Jesus offers, but Jesus' parables of the rejoicing shepherd, the woman who found her lost coin and the father waiting with a welcome-home embrace for his lost son, are pictures of Jesus celebrating because *He* has found *us*. He is planning a party to celebrate our homecoming.

The rich young man and Nicodemus were good at rule-keeping and, like many of us, they would probably have liked Jesus to give them a set of rules to keep, to ensure that they were on their way to heaven. It's ironic that Christians are caricatured as dowdy do-gooders who have to conform to a set of out-dated rules when, in fact, Jesus sets His people free from rules and regulations. Jesus, the One Christians want to be like, was criticised by the religious people of the day for spending too much time with party-people. He broke religious people's rules.

Rules make people feel safe, and boundaries are important, but Jesus invites us to love *Him* – not the rules. And by loving Him and wanting to please Him, paradoxically, our lives fall into line with God's rules for living. As the psalmist said, 'The boundary lines have fallen for me in pleasant places; surely I have a delightful inheritance' (Psa. 16:6).

One of the exciting aspects of falling in love is knowing that someone else is thinking about you and planning a future to include you. There's a road near our home which we call Glyndebourne Corner. We gave it that name when my husband, Adrian, and I were at that 'more than friends' stage. We were getting to know each other, privately wondering, 'Is this the person God has planned to be my partner for life?' At least they *were* private thoughts, until we were walking along that country road one day, talking about visiting Glyndebourne, which was nearby. Without missing a step, Adrian said, 'Well, we've got a lifetime!' That was the give-away. Although we had carefully avoided any talk of marriage, those few words betrayed his thoughts. He was planning a future that included me.

When Jesus said 'I go to prepare a place for you,' He meant you and me, with all our idiosyncrasies. Jesus sees beyond the train-spotter's anorak to understand why numbers and types of trains are so satisfying. He sees into the heart of the adrenaline junkie to see what needs are being met on the speeding rollercoaster. He understands what needs are met when the house-proud homemaker puts the last cushion in place and stands back to admire her handiwork. In the place He is preparing, no one will feel like an unnecessary extra. Each of us will know He has included us on purpose – not by accident. When we arrive in heaven, it won't be like one of those parties where you wander into a crowded room and wonder who to talk to or where to sit. Jesus is waiting to welcome the citizens of His heavenly kingdom – not formally, but as family. There won't be an embarrassed shuffling of seats to squeeze you in. He has already prepared a place just for you.

> ... He has included us on purpose – not by accident

There are lots of impossible questions to answer about heaven, but if Jesus' descriptions make you thirsty for more; remember: 'The Spirit and the bride say, "Come!" And let him who hears say, "Come!" Whoever is thirsty, let him come; and whoever wishes, let him take the free gift of the water of life' (Rev. 22:17).

> Nothing in my hand I bring,
> Simply to the cross I cling;
> Naked, come to Thee for dress;
> Helpless look to Thee for grace ...
> > Augustus M. Toplady, 'Rock of Ages, Cleft for Me'

NOTE

1. C.S. Lewis, *The Weight of Glory* (London: HarperCollins, 2001) p.31. Copyright © C.S. Lewis Pte Ltd 1949. Extract reprinted by permission.

8. WHERE IS HEAVEN?

> The only ultimate disaster that can befall us ... is to feel
> ourselves to be at home here on earth. As long as we are
> aliens we cannot forget our true homeland.
>
> Malcolm Muggeridge[1]

If you've travelled on the Northern Line of the London
Underground, you'll have heard the announcement at Old
Street station; 'Alight here for Moorfields Eye Hospital'.
Imagine travelling on the train with someone who has
been blind from birth, but with a curable eye disease.
I heard the story of someone just like that, making
that journey. He was only a boy. Everything about him
suggested he had arrived in England recently from a poor
country. His guardian was taking him to Moorfields, and
he was full of questions. He wasn't interested in specific
directions on how to get there: use exit eight at Old Street
station, follow the green painted line and access the
building via Cayton Street, which is the first turning on
your left, a further forty metres heading north down City
Road ... Those details were irrelevant to him. He was
confident that his guardian would get him safely to the
hospital. His only concern was that, once there, he would
meet the surgeon who was going to make it possible for
him to see.

In many ways it's the same with heaven. There's no
route map. Getting to heaven is about being confident
in knowing who is taking you and how you will be
transformed when you arrive.

For another way of looking at it, think about what
happens when you send a parcel as a special birthday
present: you don't know the route via postal vans and
sorting offices, but you choose a reliable delivery service

and, by addressing the parcel properly with an accurate postcode, you can be confident that it will arrive. That said, it's the delight of the person receiving the present that you are really focused on when you post the parcel. As long as it gets there, the route doesn't matter.

When Jesus taught His disciples how to talk to their heavenly Father, He said:

> 'This, then, is how you should pray:
> "Our Father in heaven,
> hallowed be your name,
> your kingdom come,
> your will be done
> on earth as it is in heaven."'

Matthew 6:9–10

The address He gave for His Father was 'in heaven'. If you want to know where heaven is so you can get there, the vital questions are, 'Who's taking you?', 'Does he know the way?' and 'Do you have an accurate address?' Not, 'What's the route?'

As for the accurate address and the heavenly 'postcode', once again that's what the Holy Spirit does in His role as 'a deposit, guaranteeing what is to come'. Just as a table-tennis ball held under water goes straight to the surface when it is released, people who have received the Holy Spirit, who have become part of God's family, are guaranteed to go straight into God's presence when they die.

But, if this is a spiritual birth, is heaven a disembodied state? Existence on a spiritual plane? When I was a child we sang a song about heaven being 'somewhere beyond the blue'. After the first space flight, the Communist leader Khrushchev delighted in saying: 'Gagarin flew into space, but didn't see any God there.' We know that

God's heavenly home is not visible in our universe, but that doesn't mean God doesn't exist or that heaven is just a spiritual state.

Back to the patterns, themes and truths revealed in the Bible. When God wanted to make an image of Himself, He made Adam – a person in flesh and blood. When He wanted to reveal Himself, Jesus became flesh and blood. When He devised a way for us to remember Him, He choose a meal and said that the ordinary bread and wine at the table were to remind us of His very real flesh and blood. After He had been crucified and had defeated death, He was once again flesh and blood: a Man who could be touched and who ate breakfast. Central to Christianity is the fact that Jesus was fully God and fully – flesh and blood – human. His resurrection was not just spiritual – His flesh and blood body was resurrected. After the resurrection, Jesus 'was taken up to heaven' as a body, and He will return in His flesh and blood body.

Being a body, as well as a mind and soul or spirit, is a crucial part of being a Christian. Our faith is worked out through communities of people described as the 'Body of Christ' – alias the Church. Our faith is recognised by what we do – bodily. And we expect to have bodies in heaven. Greek philosophers thought that bodies were inferior, so sought to transcend bodily experiences. In doing so, they also dismissed women as all body with no brain or spiritual capacity! But the Bible is quite clear, as Paul said: 'We will all be changed, so that we will never die again. Our dead and decaying bodies will be changed into bodies that won't die or decay' (1 Cor. 15:52–53, CEV).

We will have bodies in heaven, so we can conclude that heaven is a physical *place* for our bodies to be.

Back, again, to the Bible patterns: places are important to God. God has made a habit of meeting with His people and making those places special. In Genesis we read about God 'walking in the garden in the cool of the day', calling for Adam. As the Israelites travelled through the desert on their way to the promised land, God told them to make a 'Tent of Meeting' and God said, 'There I will meet you and speak to you ... and the place will be consecrated by my glory' (Exod. 29:42–43). It wasn't so much the place that was special – it was a tent which could be moved. Neither was it made sacred by its elaborate God-inspired decoration; it was special because it was inhabited by God's glory, seen visible as a cloud by day and fire at night.

When we pray 'your kingdom come, your will be done on earth as it is in heaven', we are asking God to make our lives embassies of heaven. A British embassy is a tiny piece of Britain in a foreign country. When we ask for God's kingdom to come, we are inviting God to set up an embassy in our lives. Jesus lived and breathed that prayer – that's why He could tell His disciples 'the kingdom of God has come to you' because He was with them as an ambassador of heaven. An ambassador speaks and acts on behalf of the sovereign. Jesus' mission on earth was to preach 'the good news of the kingdom'. His words were backed up by kingdom actions: '... healing every disease and sickness among the people' (Matt. 4:23).

Jesus' kingdom-bringing manifesto was:

... to preach good news to the poor.
... to proclaim freedom for the prisoners
and recovery of sight for the blind,
to release the oppressed,
to proclaim the year of the Lord's favour.'

Luke 4:18–19

He did this because 'The Spirit of the Lord is on me, because he has anointed me ...' He gives Christians the same job – to be ambassadors of the kingdom of heaven on earth. Ambassadors show their country in its best light and, in emergencies, they give safe passage home to their own citizens. The focus of all Jesus' activity was not to issue emergency tickets for heaven, but to reveal God's glory, although He does ensure that citizens of God's kingdom have access to their heavenly home.

> ... every encounter with God offers a taste of heaven

So, although the Bible suggests that heaven is a place, in some ways, the kingdom of heaven is also here – every encounter with God offers a taste of heaven. But God has also promised that there is more to come. There will be a new heaven and a new earth. According to Hebrews 1:10–12, creating a new earth will be as simple for God as rolling up an old, worn out shirt and changing it for a new one.

The prophet Isaiah looked forward to that day when God says: '... I will create new heavens and a new earth. The former things will not be remembered, nor will they come to mind' (Isa. 65:17).

John also looked forward to the new heaven and earth in his apocalyptic vision:

> Then I saw a new heaven and a new earth, for the first heaven and the first earth had passed away, and there was no longer any sea. I saw the Holy City, the new Jerusalem, coming down out of heaven from God, prepared as a bride beautifully dressed for her husband. And I heard a loud voice from the throne saying, 'Now the dwelling of God is with men, and he will live with them. They will

be his people, and God himself will be with them and be their God. He will wipe every tear from their eyes. There will be no more death or mourning or crying or pain, for the old order of things has passed away.'

Revelation 21:1–4

Two things to note in this age to come: there is still 'heaven' and 'earth'; God is still in heaven – but there is no separation between God and His people. As I love the sea, I have always found the reference to 'no more sea' to be odd, almost sad, as the sea is so beautiful. But in the imagery of the Bible the sea represents separation – and there is no separation in the age to come. God lives with us in our new, permanent home – a new earth.

If we are drawing on Bible patterns to know where a new earth will be and what it will be like, perhaps the patterns of the old covenant and new covenant give some clues. The old covenant involved animal sacrifices and related to a specific group of people. Under the new covenant all the symbols of the old covenant were fulfilled in Jesus, who became the once-for-all sacrifice.

He is looking forward to celebrating with us

Jesus taught His disciples to use bread and wine to look back to what His death had achieved – and to look forward: 'For whenever you eat this bread and drink this cup, you proclaim the Lord's death until he comes' (1 Cor. 11:26).

At the Last Supper, Jesus said, '… I will not drink of this fruit of the vine from now on until that day when I drink it anew with you in my Father's kingdom' (Matt. 26:29). He is looking forward to celebrating with us.

When God makes something new, He seems to take

the old patterns and builds on them – the result has shadows of the old, but is entirely new. We can expect the new earth to resemble what we know. Imagine explaining music to a deaf child. She can feel the rhythms, but can only imagine what music is like. The best this earth can offer is an impression of the new earth God has planned. The real thing is unimaginable.

The Great Divorce, C.S. Lewis's profound analogy about the journey to heaven, might help here. The characters in the story find themselves on a bus journey from the twilight world in which we now live. At their destination, the passengers get out of the bus into 'a larger sort of space, than I had ever known before ... I had got "out" in some sense which made the Solar System itself seem as an indoor affair'.

In this place 'the light, the grass, the trees, were different; made of some different substance, so much solider than things in our country that men were ghosts by comparison'.

As the story unfolds, the ghost of a woman called Pam meets a 'Bright Spirit' who is one of the residents of this country. Her goal is to meet her son Michael, who has already arrived in this intoxicatingly beautiful place. Her problem is that, like everything from the world we know, she is so insubstantial, her son would not be able to see her even if she did meet him. 'You'd be totally invisible to Michael,' the Bright Spirit tells her, 'You need to be thickened up a bit.'

'How?' said the Ghost ...

'The first step is a hard one,' said the Spirit. 'But after that you'll get on like a house on fire. You will become solid enough for Michael to perceive you when you learn to want Someone Else besides Michael ... It's only a little germ of a desire for God that we need to start the process.'

'Oh, you mean religion and all that sort of thing? This is hardly the moment … and from *you*, of all people. Well, never mind, I'll do whatever's necessary. What do you want me to do? Come on. The sooner I begin it, the sooner they'll let me see my boy. I'm quite ready.'

'But, Pam, do think! Don't you see you are not beginning at all as long as you are in that state of mind? You're treating God only as a means to Michael. But the whole thickening treatment consists of learning to want God for His own sake.'[2]

In C.S. Lewis's imagination, heaven is a more substantial place than we can imagine. It's as different from the world we know as real people are from two-dimensional cartoon characters. Getting there isn't about doing the right things, following rules or a route map; it's about responding to God's love, starting a relationship with Him, longing for more of Him … more of His presence. It's a growing relationship that will one day become a completely different and much more substantial reality.

> Getting there isn't about doing the right things …

One more picture: in Jesus' time, when a young man wanted to get married, he told his father first. If his father approved, the son would start to build a home attached to his father's house. Then the young man would go to his bride-to-be and say something like, 'In my house there is room for you. I am preparing a place, and when my father tells me it is finished to his standards, I will come to get you. Then we will be together.'

When Jesus told His disciples about heaven, He was using images and concepts they already knew and building on them to explain where heaven can be found. He said:

> Do not let your hearts be troubled. Trust in God; trust also in me. In my Father's house are many rooms; if it were not so, I would have told you. I am going there to prepare a place for you. And if I go and prepare a place for you, I will come back and take you to be with me that you also may be where I am.
>
> John 14:1–3

He says the same to His contemporary disciples – His bride-to-be. Where is heaven? It is where our heavenly Father lives; where Jesus is preparing a place for those who respond to His love.

> It is not darkness you are going to, for God is Light. It is not lonely, for Christ is with you. It is not unknown country, for Christ is there.
>
> Charles Kingsley

NOTES

1. Malcolm Muggeridge, *Jesus Rediscovered* (Fount, 1969) pp.17–18.
2. C.S. Lewis, *The Great Divorce* (Fount, 2002). Copyright © C.S. Lewis Pte Ltd 1946. Extract reprinted by permission.

WHEN –

AFTER LIFE OR HERE AND NOW?

9. WHEN – AFTER LIFE OR HERE AND NOW?

I look forward to death with colossal joy.

Malcolm Muggeridge

… and they all lived happily ever after. Isn't that how we long for our story to end? When God made the world, death and decay had no part in it. But once sin began to corrupt the perfect world God had created, He had to put limits on the spread of evil. Sometimes good things need to be stopped, before they turn bad – like ripe fruit that needs to be picked before it's past its best. That's why death can be described as God's mercy.

Sin separates people from God now and eternally, but heaven promises beginnings without endings: no death, no separation, but life and joy and peace in abundance. Words like 'satisfied', 'whole', 'complete' and 'full' are used to describe the experience of heaven.

In the gloomy days of the 1930s Depression, Ginger Rogers and Fred Astaire struck a chord with this song:

Heaven … I'm in heaven
And my heart beats so that I can hardly speak.
And I seem to find the happiness I seek,
When we're out together dancing cheek to cheek.[1]

People in the thirties were hungry for heaven and the song resonated with the desires of cinema audiences who longed to escape the dreariness of life, dancing with apparently effortless ease to the crooning love songs of the age. Heaven was finding happiness in the arms of your one true love.

Certainly, heaven is something to look forward to

after this life is over. Jesus talked a great deal about the kingdom of heaven, His coming kingdom. He taught His disciples to pray: 'your kingdom come . . .' But when some Pharisees asked Jesus *when* God's kingdom would come, Jesus answered: 'God's kingdom isn't something you can see. There is no use saying, "Look! Here it is" or "Look! There it is." God's kingdom is here with you' (Luke 17:20–21, CEV). That suggests heaven is now as well as not yet, and it is more to do with God's presence with us than our destination.

When Jesus prayed for His followers, He said:

> I pray . . . that all of them may be one, Father, just as you are in me and I am in you. May they also be in us so that the world may believe that you have sent me. I have given them the glory that you gave me, that they may be one as we are one . . .'

John 17:20–22

When a sponge is submerged in a bucket of water, you can say 'the sponge is in the water' but also 'the water is in the sponge'. There's a mind-bending aspect of heaven in which we become integrated with God. We don't escape into a new reality, nor are we absorbed into some spiritual realm – we are bodies, remember. But we become more fully what we were created to be – and the process starts as soon as the Holy Spirit begins His work in our lives.

When the Holy Spirit comes to live in us, we meet with God – and other people can meet with Him too, because of us. Just as Moses' face shone after he had met with God, Christians reflect God's glory to the world around. What makes heaven special is that 'the dwelling of God is with men, and he will live with them' (Rev. 21:3). Heaven comes when God is present. As God's people,

Christians bring a taste of heaven into the world when they campaign for justice, reach out in compassion or call for integrity and truth.

When we pray the Lord's Prayer, we normally add words about God's glory to the end of the prayer: 'For the kingdom, the power and the glory are yours, now and for ever. Amen.' Although they were not part of the original prayer that Jesus taught His disciples, these words remind us that the focus of a Christian's life is not 'pie in the sky when you die', but bringing glory to God – now and forever.

> Christians reflect God's glory to the world around

That's what Jesus was talking about when He asked His Father: '... I want those you have given me to be with me where I am, and to see my glory, the glory you have given me because you loved me before the creation of the world' (John 17:24).

In this life, we see only a glimpse of God's glory. But, as C.S. Lewis said: 'What would it be to taste at the fountain-head that stream of which even the lower reaches prove so intoxicating? Yet that, I believe is what lies before us.'[2]

What is God's glory? The apostle Paul said, '... we, who with unveiled faces all reflect the Lord's glory, are being transformed into his likeness with ever-increasing glory, which comes from the Lord, who is the Spirit' (2 Cor. 3:18).

God's glory is revealed in unexpected places. In 1973 Bishop Festo Kivengere saw God's glory revealed when three men from his diocese faced a government firing squad on a trumped-up charge. In an article in *African Saints: Saints, Martyrs, and Holy People from the Continent of Africa*, Frederick Quinn quotes the Bishop's description of the execution:

February 10 began as a sad day for us in Kabale. People were commanded to come to the stadium and witness the execution. Death permeated the atmosphere. A silent crowd of about three thousand was there ready to watch. I had permission from the authorities to speak to the men before they died, and two of my fellow ministers were with me. They brought the men in a truck and unloaded them. They were handcuffed and their feet were chained. The firing squad stood at attention. As we walked into the center of the stadium, I was wondering what to say. How do you give the Gospel to doomed men who are probably seething with rage?

We approached them from behind, and as they turned to look at us, what a sight! Their faces were all alight with an unmistakable glow and radiance. Before we could say anything, one of them burst out: 'Bishop, thank you for coming! I wanted to tell you. The day I was arrested, in my prison cell, I asked the Lord Jesus to come into my heart. He came in and forgave me all my sins! Heaven is now open, and there is nothing between me and my God! Please tell my wife and children that I am going to be with Jesus. Ask them to accept him into their lives as I did.' The other two men told similar stories, excitedly raising their hands, which rattled their handcuffs.

I felt that what I needed to do was to talk to the soldiers, not to the condemned. So I translated what the men had said into a language the soldiers understood. The military men were standing there with guns cocked and bewilderment on their faces. They were so dumbfounded that they forgot to put the hoods over the men's faces! The three faced the firing squad standing close together. They looked toward the people and began to wave, handcuffs and all. The people waved back. Then shots were fired, and the three were with Jesus.[3]

That crowd saw the glory of God. Those three men had a taste of heaven even before they met their Maker. For them, heaven opened. Their deaths were not separation, but consummation.

Christians believe that they have already died to their old way of life and have begun a new life as part of Christ. As the apostle Paul explained to the Colossians: 'For you died, and your life is now hidden with Christ in God. When Christ, who is your life, appears, then you also will appear with him in glory' (Col. 3:3–4).

> That crowd saw the glory of God

The New Testament letters are shot though with this paradox: heaven is now and not yet. As Mother Teresa of Calcutta said:

> We all long for heaven where God is but we have it in our power to be in heaven with Him right now, to be happy with Him at this very moment. But being happy with Him now means: Loving as He loves; Helping as He helps; Giving as He gives; Serving as He serves; Rescuing as He rescues; Being with Him for all the 24 hours; touching Him in His dangerous disguises.

NOTES

1. Irving Berlin, 'Cheek to Cheek'.
2. C.S. Lewis, *Screwtape Proposes a Toast* (Fount, 1998). Copyright © C.S. Lewis Pte Ltd 1959. Extract reprinted by permission.
3. Frederick Quinn, 'Festo Kivengere', *African Saints: Saints, Martyrs, and Holy People from the Continent of Africa* (New York: Crossroads Publishing Company, 2002). The full article can be found at http://www.dacb.org/stories/uganda/kivengere_festo.html. Used with permission of the Dictionary of African Christian Biography, 490 Prospect Street, New Haven, CT 06511-2196 USA. http://www.dacb.org

10. HOW DO I LIVE NOW?

> The term is over: the holidays have begun. The dream is ended: this is the morning ... All their life in this world and their adventures in Narnia had only been the cover and the title page: now at last they were beginning Chapter One of the great Story which no one on earth has read: which goes on forever: in which every chapter is better than the one before.
>
> C.S. Lewis[1]

Vision is a picture of the future that produces passion in the present and gives meaning to otherwise meaningless tasks, says my friend Sandy Medway. She founded a charity to help people find meaningful work, which matches their skills and interests – so she's seen this pithy prose in practice. It's amazing what you can do when you have a vision of where you want to be. That's how apprentices can show their dedication as they do menial tasks. For me as a trainee journalist, the goal of writing for a living meant I persevered with the more menial task of writing seemingly endless local newspaper reports on funerals and flower shows; but what does it mean for apprentices in God's service? What vision motivates Christians?

As we have seen in the previous chapters, we were made for heaven – revealed in the Bible as a fruitful garden, a royal dwelling place – as awesome as a throne room and as intimate as a bridal suite. We can look forward to a celebration, a wedding, a victory parade and our final homecoming. But there is more to the vision which spurs Christians on through persecution, emotional and spiritual deserts, and through all manner of pain and hardship. An empty heaven is not enough – heaven only becomes worth reaching because the one who loves us is there. It is that love relationship which draws Christians forward. Getting to heaven isn't about doing the right things or following rules, it's about responding to God's love and developing a lasting, loving relationship with Him.

... as awesome as a throne room and as intimate as a bridal suite

Jesus told a graphic story about sheep and goats, recorded by Matthew. The 'sheep' in His story received a place in His heavenly kingdom: they fed the hungry, welcomed strangers, clothed the naked, cared for sick people and visited prisoners. In serving others, Jesus said they were serving Him. How does that square with the fact that good deeds don't get people into heaven? If you read the story in Matthew 25, you'll see that loving and serving was instinctive for those who were given a place in heaven. They were not trying to earn Brownie points – their good deeds reflected their unselfish love and care for the people around them. They had been transformed by God's love and, as a result, they loved others and those touched by them tasted heaven.

But practical love and care for others didn't come naturally to the 'goats'. They ignored people who were hungry, thirsty, naked, sick and in prison. Jesus said that was tantamount to ignoring Him. These 'goats' might have said they were Jesus' followers, but they had not been transformed by His love to become people who love others ... that oneness and integration with Jesus that we looked at in the last chapter, hadn't happened to them. They weren't being ambassadors of heaven – the people they met were not tasting heaven by being with them.

Becoming 'sheep', rather than 'goats' isn't something

that can be achieved by sheer hard work and willpower – it's all about responding to God's love. When you love someone you change in lots of ways: it might mean crossing continents to be with them – or squeezing the toothpaste tube differently. But God's apprentices are more than mere servants following orders or rules, they are adopted into God's family. The life of God surges through them and they display the family's characteristics without even thinking about it, in the most menial task and in every aspect of life.

The journey to the kingdom is more of a romance than a route-march; a response of love rather than an act of willpower. It's about being united with Christ – becoming one with Him, now and forever … easy words to write, but an awesome mystery, which will only be revealed in eternity.

Until then we wait, like lovers longing to be in each other's arms. Heaven is beyond anything we can anticipate. We can only guess at what it will mean to be with Christ in the home He is preparing for us.

As I've sought to write this short book, I know that words are inadequate; stories and parables can only give glimpses of heaven – there is so much we cannot know. But, we have a lifetime, an eternal lifetime, to discover what Paul was talking about when he prayed:

> … that you, being rooted and established in love, may have power, together with all the saints, to grasp how wide and long and high and deep is the love of Christ, and to know this love that surpasses knowledge – that you may be filled to the measure of all the fullness of God.
>
> Now to him who is able to do immeasurably more than all we ask or imagine, according to his power that is at work within us, to him be glory in the church and

in Christ Jesus throughout all generations, for ever and ever! Amen.

Ephesians 3:17–21

That's my prayer for you as you finish reading this brief introduction to heaven. As you think back over the images of heaven we've considered in this book, allow God to stir you. Listen to your heart's cries. Identify the true source of your longings in life. Allow God to quench your thirst – to satisfy your appetite for more. Ask Him to give you a clearer vision of an eternal future with Christ. Let that put the rest of you life into perspective. As Paul said,

Therefore we do not lose heart. Though outwardly we are wasting away, yet inwardly we are being renewed day by day. For our light and momentary troubles are achieving for us an eternal glory that far outweighs them all. So we fix our eyes not on what is seen, but on what is unseen. For what is seen is temporary, but what is unseen is eternal.

2 Corinthians 4:16–18

NOTE
1. C.S. Lewis, *The Last Battle* (Lions, 1980) p.172. Copyright © C.S. Lewis Pte Ltd 1956. Extract reprinted by permission.

NATIONAL DISTRIBUTORS

UK: (and countries not listed below)
CWR, Waverley Abbey House, Waverley Lane, Farnham, Surrey GU9 8EP.
Tel: (01252) 784700 Outside UK (44) 1252 784700

AUSTRALIA: CMC Australasia, PO Box 519, Belmont, Victoria 3216.
Tel: (03) 5241 3288 Fax: (03) 5241 3290

CANADA: Cook Communications Ministries, PO Box 98, 55 Woodslee Avenue,
Paris, Ontario N3L 3E5. Tel: 1800 263 2664

GHANA: Challenge Enterprises of Ghana, PO Box 5723, Accra.
Tel: (021) 222437/223249 Fax: (021) 226227

HONG KONG: Cross Communications Ltd, 1/F, 562A Nathan Road, Kowloon.
Tel: 2780 1188 Fax: 2770 6229

INDIA: Crystal Communications, 10-3-18/4/1, East Marredpalli, Secunderabad
– 500026, Andhra Pradesh. Tel/Fax: (040) 27737145

KENYA: Keswick Books and Gifts Ltd, PO Box 10242, Nairobi.
Tel: (02) 331692/226047 Fax: (02) 728557

MALAYSIA: Salvation Book Centre (M) Sdn Bhd, 23 Jalan SS 2/64, 47300 Petaling
Jaya, Selangor. Tel: (03) 78766411/78766797 Fax: (03) 78757066/78756360

NEW ZEALAND: CMC Australasia, PO Box 303298, North Harbour, Auckland
0751. Tel: 0800 449 408 Fax: 0800 449 049

NIGERIA: FBFM, Helen Baugh House, 96 St Finbarr's College Road, Akoka, Lagos.
Tel: (01) 7747429/4700218/825775/827264

PHILIPPINES: OMF Literature Inc, 776 Boni Avenue, Mandaluyong City.
Tel: (02) 531 2183 Fax: (02) 531 1960

SINGAPORE: Alby Commercial Enterprises Pte Ltd, 95 Kallang Avenue #04-00,
AIS Industrial Building, 339420. Tel: (65) 629 27238 Fax: (65) 629 27235

SOUTH AFRICA: Struik Christian Books, 80 MacKenzie Street, PO Box 1144,
Cape Town 8000. Tel: (021) 462 4360 Fax: (021) 461 3612

SRI LANKA: Christombu Publications (Pvt) Ltd, Bartleet House, 65 Braybrooke
Place, Colombo 2. Tel: (9411) 2421073/2447665

TANZANIA: CLC Christian Book Centre, PO Box 1384, Mkwepu Street, Dar es
Salaam. Tel/Fax: (022) 2119439

USA: Cook Communications Ministries, PO Box 98, 55 Woodslee Avenue, Paris,
Ontario N3L 3E5, Canada. Tel: 1800 263 2664

ZIMBABWE: Word of Life Books (Pvt) Ltd, Christian Media Centre, 8 Aberdeen
Road, Avondale, PO Box A480 Avondale, Harare. Tel: (04) 333355 or 091301188

For email addresses, visit the CWR website: www.cwr.org.uk

CWR is a Registered Charity – Number 294387

**CWR is a Limited Company registered in England – Registration
Number 1990308**

Trusted all Over the World

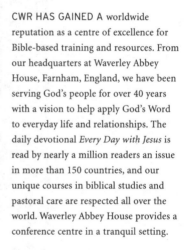

CWR HAS GAINED A worldwide reputation as a centre of excellence for Bible-based training and resources. From our headquarters at Waverley Abbey House, Farnham, England, we have been serving God's people for over 40 years with a vision to help apply God's Word to everyday life and relationships. The daily devotional *Every Day with Jesus* is read by nearly a million readers an issue in more than 150 countries, and our unique courses in biblical studies and pastoral care are respected all over the world. Waverley Abbey House provides a conference centre in a tranquil setting.

For free brochures on our seminars and courses, conference facilities, or a catalogue of CWR resources, please contact us at the following address: **CWR, Waverley Abbey House, Waverley Lane, Farnham, Surrey GU9 8EP, UK**

Telephone: **+44 (0)1252 784700**
Email: **mail@cwr.org.uk**
Website: **www.cwr.org.uk**

 Applying God's Word
to everyday life and relationships

WHAT YOU ALWAYS WANTED TO KNOW ABOUT PRAYER ... BUT WERE AFRAID TO ASK

IAN COFFEY

Ian Coffey, well-known Christian speaker, author and church leader, provides answers to the most frequently asked questions about prayer. The book also includes short testimonies from other well-known Christians, including Rosemary Conley, Graham Kendrick and Rob Frost.

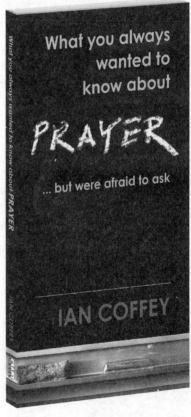

ISBN: 978-1-85345-415-8
£7.99

Price correct at time of printing.